Top Squawk

9465 W Post Road
Bldg. #19 Suite 2037
Las Vegas Nevada 89148
917-881-2172
Win817105@hotmail.com

Registered WGAE
2006

Visit www.booksurge.com to order additional copies.

JOHN P. DE MEO

TOP SQUAWK

NEW YORK TRADING
FLOOR QUOTES

2007

Top Squawk

For Eddy, Elkin and Ed. Your smiles remain with us.

"He threw me under the bus!" or "I was thrown under the bus!"

Blamed for something that may or may not be true, in order to shift responsibility.

"You cheap, selfish idiot! You made so much money last year that they had to deliver your 1099 with a crane."

A response from one broker to another who was complaining about having a losing day.

"It's either going to trade higher or we will make a new low"

The ultimate market opinion.

"Let me get this straight, you want to check this order? The only way that this order even has a shot at being filled is if they find oil in Central Park!"

A response to a trader checking an order that was way below the market.

"You are eating too many onions!"

One broker explaining to another why the gold chain that he sold him is turning his neck green.

"Look at you! Your complexion could inspire a new crayon color."

A conversation between clerks.

"He has stage three broker dementia!"

The reason given for the behavior of a gray haired "Dead Head" broker who enjoys running up to visitors on the trading floor and startling them by screaming SOLD in their faces.

"Just boil it all Patty! Boil it all!"

Yelled seconds before the Mayor of Dublin opened our crude oil market.

"I heard that you quit. Is it true?"
"Quit what?"
"The circus, you freak!"

The floor attracts "unique" individuals.

"Take a look at the size of Mike's head and answer me this, would you rather have his head full of nickels or a million bucks?"

The size of the head speaks for itself.

"I told you, don't drink and trade!"

Advice from a floor manager to a broker angry over an order executed backwards.

"He is not the sharpest marble in the jar."

A person who is not a standout on the trading floor, but is probably more street smart than most people in the outside world.

"Listen, I know that you are not the sharpest knife in the drawer."

You better hope that the floor does not go electronic. Too late!

"Who was this order for? It has no code on it."
"I hope that you did a good job, because it's for you, midget!"

A retaliatory set up after months of arguing. Explaining why an order was not customer coded, essentially telling the executing broker that he now has a large position for his own account and risk. Upon hearing this, the broker ran from the pit and choked the phone clerk who set him up. It took five people to separate them.

"Tighten me up!"

A request for gum, candy or food that was snuck onto the trading floor.

"This would be a great way to make a living if it wasn't for the customers."

A broker's response to a difficult customer order request.

"What do you think that this is? Wait! I know what this is! It's a telethon to raise money for my anxiety medication!"

The ranting of a broker while the market is frenzied and every phone in the booth is ringing off the hook.

"What can I say? I did the best that I could."

A broker's explanation on why he sold the low of the market's closing range.

"My trades are so bad today that I can't catch a cold."

It is time to stop trading for the day.

"I have some advice for you. I have been in this business for over seventeen years, and I have learned to live by just four little words. Trust only the dead."

Advice given to me on my first day by a veteran broker.

"Oh my God! Oh my God!"
"What does oh my God mean?"
"It should have been a sale, sell, sell, sell!"

An exchange between a clerk and a broker regarding a large error that ultimately cost $270,000.

"Hurry up and check this trade with me, I have mud in my pants!"

No translation necessary.

"I am so right today that I am printing money!"

Press the streak until it ends, and take the profits.

"You can never go broke taking profits."

Widely heard but not necessarily true, your profits have to add up to more than your losses. Good traders ride their winners, and cut their losses by exiting bad positions.

"Where is the bid?"
"The bid is in your sister's pants!"

The floor is the ultimate locker room environment.

"I like that over there. She is hot. I want to take her away for a weekend"

"Hey, watch yourself. That's my sister!"

"Oh, I'm sorry about that, I apologize, I really didn't know."

"I guess I should have said that about those two big girls over there"

"Now you are really getting on my nerves, those are my sister's too!"

The trading floor is the best example of nepotism on earth.

"Look at you! You are the dumbest rich man in commodities!"

This is not the Big Board, these people are the stepchildren of Wall Street.

"I took customers to a strip club last night, and I met this stripper. I think that I'm in love. She is so hot that I would leave my wife and girlfriend for her. I mean, I want to dig a dungeon for her in my backyard."

Everyman has his own concept of love.

"What's trading?"

When someone has food on the trading floor the aroma causes the guys to circle like sharks that have smelled blood in the water.

"Cheers!"

What almost every London customer says before he hangs up the phone.

"Ten seconds!"

As everyone on the floor waits with anticipation, right before the market opens the ring announcer yells over the microphone.

"Look at you! Jackie Gleason bowling shirt wearing, Andy Garcia hair slicked sporting, Stallone pumped looking, De Niro mole wearing, do you get confused? I mean do you have an identity crisis?"

Are these observations or compliments? A little of both I guess.

"Our clocks are one minute off. So today, we will close one minute early, so that we are the same as the outside world."

This announcement illustrates the mindset of separateness; the floor is its own world.

"You got any interest?"

May apply to trading or a sexual suggestion.

"I'm a buyer!"

A floor person likes something; it could be the market or anything else, the equivalent of bullish.

"I'm a seller!"

A floor person who dislikes something; the equivalent of bearish.

"Show size!"

A request to know the size of a bid or offer; may also have a sexual meaning.

"We have buyers, we have sellers, and we have lots of happy fellas!"

A response to the President of a large Wall Street brokerage firm who called the trading floor in order to find out why the oil market was so volatile on a particular trading day. Subsequently, the person who used this gem was fired. Rumor has it that he has been in a Mexican jail for eight years.

"We were crop dusted!"

When a person on the floor walks out of his usual work area to fart and returns to watch those who have been "crop dusted" as they cover up their mouths and noses because they cannot move from where they are standing.

"Bag a bucks! Bag a bucks!"
A game in which a female clerk walks around yelling
"bag a bucks" collecting five dollar bills for deposit
in a bag. The people participating write their names
on the bills and the person who has their bill picked
wins the contents. (Less a tip of course)

"We listened to the tapes. It was a cluster job."

A situation in which multiple errors were made on the same trade, usually by more than one person involved. This is determined by listening to the taped phone lines.

"I have such big swings now that it's like funny money."

A local trader commenting on the immense amount of capital required to trade the current extremely volatile energy futures markets. This is almost "unreal" to veteran traders.

"Reeeda! Reeeda! Reeeda!" (Broker Badge Chant)

For years, this chant was made for one of the brokers at the same time on Friday afternoons by hundreds on the floor.

"One more order! Just one more order! If you guys give me one more order I am walking out! I mean it! We have three brokers in this pit! One more order, give it to me! Give it to me! Just do it! Do it!"

This was screamed during the mayhem that ensued after the weekly petroleum inventory numbers were released vastly differing from expectations.

"That's all! That's all! That's all! The market is closed!"

As the closing buzzer sounds, that's it!

Favorite Movie Quotes of the trading floor.

Goodfellas

"Forget about tonight."

"I thought that I told you to go get your shine box!"

"I took care of that thing for you."

The Godfather

"It's what Pop wanted! It wasn't what I wanted! I'm smart!"

"Cheech! Abort!"

Inspired by; "Just think, if they had EZ pass back in the day, Sonny would still be alive."

JOHN P. DE MEO

The Pope of Greenwich Village

"Charlie! They took my thumb!"

Raging Bull

"Bring it over!"

"Coffee! Coffee!"

"You never got me down Ray!"

As Jake La Motta opened our crude oil market.

Things to Do in Denver When You're Dead

"He's crazy as an outhouse rat!"

Glengarry GlenRoss

"Never open your mouth until you know what the shot is!"

"I'm going to find out whose nephew you are!"

Trading Places

"Turn those machines back on!"